THE Black Book

Copyright: © 2016 Sandra Borchert, Oxana Henkel
Herstellung und Verlag: BoD – Books on Demand
Norderstedt

ISBN 978–3–7412-6645-4

Name:

Relationship status:

Phone:

Facebook:

Skype:

Body:

Eye colour:

Hair colour:

Tattoo:

Piercing:

Favourite Drink:

Favourite Food:

Favourite Car:

Favourite Music:

Favourite Movie:

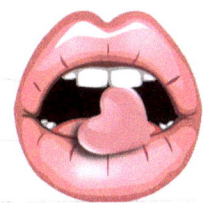

Children:

First Date:

First Kiss:

First Night:

He is good at:

He is bad at:

What do I want:

Dad likes him:

Will I call him again:

Will I date him again:

Rate him: ★★★★★

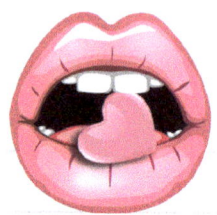

Name:

Relationship status:

Phone:

Facebook:

Skype:

Body:

Eye colour:

Hair colour:

Tattoo:

Piercing:

Favourite Drink:

Favourite Food:

Favourite Car:

Favourite Music:

Favourite Movie:

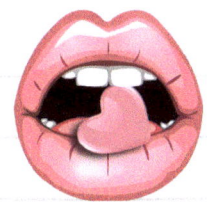

Children:

First Date:

First Kiss:

First Night:

He is good at:

He is bad at:

What do I want:

Dad likes him:

Will I call him again:

Will I date him again:

Rate him: ☆☆☆☆☆

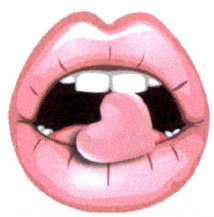

Name:

Relationship status:

Phone:

Facebook:

Skype:

Body:

Eye colour:

Hair colour:

Tattoo:

Piercing:

Favourite Drink:

Favourite Food:

Favourite Car:

Favourite Music:

Favourite Movie:

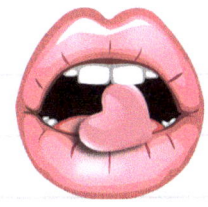

Children:

First Date:

First Kiss:

First Night:

He is good at:

He is bad at:

What do I want:

Dad likes him:

Will I call him again:

Will I date him again:

Rate him: ★★★★★

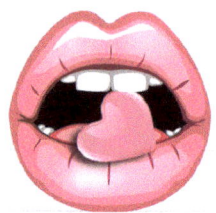

Name:

Relationship status:

Phone:

Facebook:

Skype:

Body:

Eye colour:

Hair colour:

Tattoo:

Piercing:

Favourite Drink:

Favourite Food:

Favourite Car:

Favourite Music:

Favourite Movie:

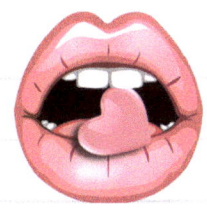

Children:

First Date:

First Kiss:

First Night:

He is good at:

He is bad at:

What do I want:

Dad likes him:

Will I call him again:

Will I date him again:

Rate him: ☆☆☆☆☆

Name:

Relationship status:

Phone:

Facebook:

Skype:

Body:

Eye colour:

Hair colour:

Tattoo:

Piercing:

Favourite Drink:

Favourite Food:

Favourite Car:

Favourite Music:

Favourite Movie:

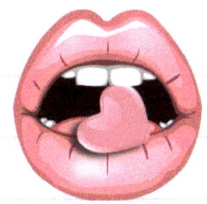

Children:

First Date:

First Kiss:

First Night:

He is good at:

He is bad at:

What do I want:

Dad likes him:

Will I call him again:

Will I date him again:

Rate him: ★★★★★

Name:

Relationship status:

Phone:

Facebook:

Skype:

Body:

Eye colour:

Hair colour:

Tattoo:

Piercing:

Favourite Drink:

Favourite Food:

Favourite Car:

Favourite Music:

Favourite Movie:

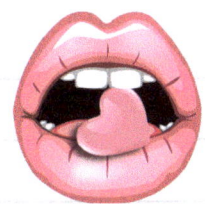

Children:

First Date:

First Kiss:

First Night:

He is good at:

He is bad at:

What do I want:

Dad likes him:

Will I call him again:

Will I date him again:

Rate him: ★★★★★

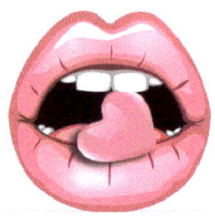

Name:

Relationship status:

Phone:

Facebook:

Skype:

Body:

Eye colour:

Hair colour:

Tattoo:

Piercing:

Favourite Drink:

Favourite Food:

Favourite Car:

Favourite Music:

Favourite Movie:

Children:

First Date:

First Kiss:

First Night:

He is good at:

He is bad at:

What do I want:

Dad likes him:

Will I call him again:

Will I date him again:

Rate him: ★★★★★

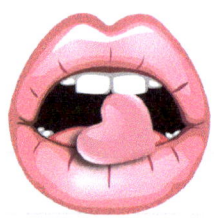

Name:

Relationship status:

Phone:

Facebook:

Skype:

Body:

Eye colour:

Hair colour:

Tattoo:

Piercing:

Favourite Drink:

Favourite Food:

Favourite Car:

Favourite Music:

Favourite Movie:

Children:

First Date:

First Kiss:

First Night:

He is good at:

He is bad at:

What do I want:

Dad likes him:

Will I call him again:

Will I date him again:

Rate him: ☆☆☆☆☆

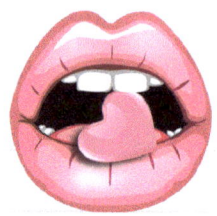

Name:

Relationship status:

Phone:

Facebook:

Skype:

Body:

Eye colour:

Hair colour:

Tattoo:

Piercing:

Favourite Drink:

Favourite Food:

Favourite Car:

Favourite Music:

Favourite Movie:

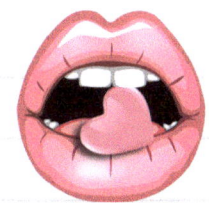

Children:

First Date:

First Kiss:

First Night:

He is good at:

He is bad at:

What do I want:

Dad likes him:

Will I call him again:

Will I date him again:

Rate him: ★★★★★

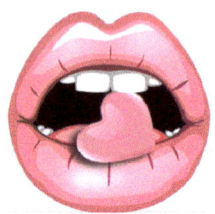

Name:

Relationship status:

Phone:

Facebook:

Skype:

Body:

Eye colour:

Hair colour:

Tattoo:

Piercing:

Favourite Drink:

Favourite Food:

Favourite Car:

Favourite Music:

Favourite Movie:

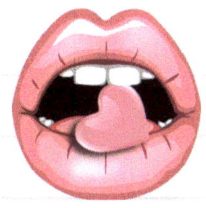

Children:

First Date:

First Kiss:

First Night:

He is good at:

He is bad at:

What do I want:

Dad likes him:

Will I call him again:

Will I date him again:

Rate him: ☆☆☆☆☆

Name:

Relationship status:

Phone:

Facebook:

Skype:

Body:

Eye colour:

Hair colour:

Tattoo:

Piercing:

Favourite Drink:

Favourite Food:

Favourite Car:

Favourite Music:

Favourite Movie:

Children:

First Date:

First Kiss:

First Night:

He is good at:

He is bad at:

What do I want:

Dad likes him:

Will I call him again:

Will I date him again:

Rate him: ★★★★★

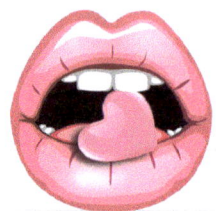

Name:

Relationship status:

Phone:

Facebook:

Skype:

Body:

Eye colour:

Hair colour:

Tattoo:

Piercing:

Favourite Drink:

Favourite Food:

Favourite Car:

Favourite Music:

Favourite Movie:

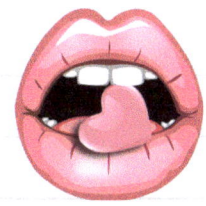

Children:

First Date:

First Kiss:

First Night:

He is good at:

He is bad at:

What do I want:

Dad likes him:

Will I call him again:

Will I date him again:

Rate him: ☆☆☆☆☆

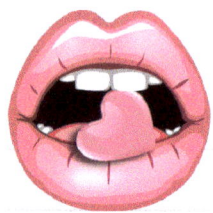

Name:

Relationship status:

Phone:

Facebook:

Skype:

Body:

Eye colour:

Hair colour:

Tattoo:

Piercing:

Favourite Drink:

Favourite Food:

Favourite Car:

Favourite Music:

Favourite Movie:

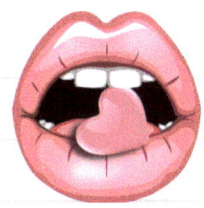

Children:

First Date:

First Kiss:

First Night:

He is good at:

He is bad at:

What do I want:

Dad likes him:

Will I call him again:

Will I date him again:

Rate him: ☆☆☆☆☆

Name:

Relationship status:

Phone:

Facebook:

Skype:

Body:

Eye colour:

Hair colour:

Tattoo:

Piercing:

Favourite Drink:

Favourite Food:

Favourite Car:

Favourite Music:

Favourite Movie:

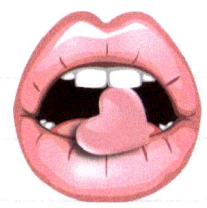

Children:

First Date:

First Kiss:

First Night:

He is good at:

He is bad at:

What do I want:

Dad likes him:

Will I call him again:

Will I date him again:

Rate him: ☆☆☆☆☆

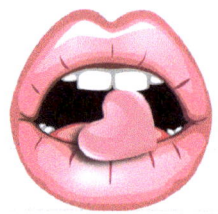

Name:

Relationship status:

Phone:

Facebook:

Skype:

Body:

Eye colour:

Hair colour:

Tattoo:

Piercing:

Favourite Drink:

Favourite Food:

Favourite Car:

Favourite Music:

Favourite Movie:

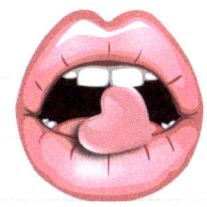

Children:

First Date:

First Kiss:

First Night:

He is good at:

He is bad at:

What do I want:

Dad likes him:

Will I call him again:

Will I date him again:

Rate him: ★★★★★

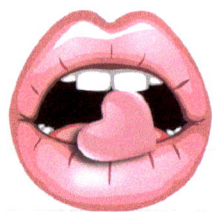

Name:

Relationship status:

Phone:

Facebook:

Skype:

Body:

Eye colour:

Hair colour:

Tattoo:

Piercing:

Favourite Drink:

Favourite Food:

Favourite Car:

Favourite Music:

Favourite Movie:

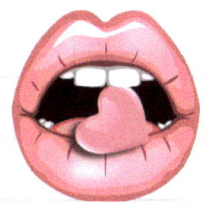

Children:

First Date:

First Kiss:

First Night:

He is good at:

He is bad at:

What do I want:

Dad likes him:

Will I call him again:

Will I date him again:

Rate him: ☆☆☆☆☆

Name:

Relationship status:

Phone:

Facebook:

Skype:

Body:

Eye colour:

Hair colour:

Tattoo:

Piercing:

Favourite Drink:

Favourite Food:

Favourite Car:

Favourite Music:

Favourite Movie:

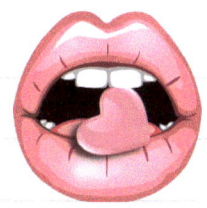

Children:

First Date:

First Kiss:

First Night:

He is good at:

He is bad at:

What do I want:

Dad likes him:

Will I call him again:

Will I date him again:

Rate him: